THE OFFICIAL
Arsenal
ANNUAL
2012

Written by Chas Newkey-Burden

A Grange Publication

TM©(2011) The Arsenal Football Club plc. All rights reserved.
Manufactured and distributed under licence by Grange
Communications Ltd., Edinburgh. Printed in the EU.

Photography © Arsenal Football Club and Action Images.

Arsenal logo and crest are registered trademarks of The Arsenal
Football Club plc.

ISBN 978-1-908221-17-9

£7.99

Contents

Manager's Message

Welcome to the Official Arsenal Annual 2012. I hope you enjoy what follows in these pages. You will find wonderful memories of the 2010/11 season, as well as other fun and fascinating features. The latest campaign was a challenging one for all. I believe we showed that we have the technical quality to win trophies but at times we lacked the strength and solidity that is required to go with it.

The team undoubtedly learned many lessons during the season but we can all reflect on some wonderful performances. Among these were the victory against Barcelona in the first-leg of our UEFA Champions League tie; high-scoring wins over Aston Villa, Shakhtar Donetsk and Blackpool; and our victory over champions-elect Manchester United in May.

I assure you that everyone at the Club is working hard and we'll try and add another trophy to Arsenal's illustrious list of honours. As Arsenal Football Club celebrates its 125th anniversary, we are all aware of the one thing that has been constant throughout that time - the support of Arsenal fans. Once again, I thank you for your inspirational support. It means a lot to the players and myself to hear you backing us through thick and thin.

Here's to the future,

Arsène Wenger
Manager

Premier League Review

It was one of the most competitive league campaigns for some time. The Gunners were rarely short of goals and excitement as they provided the usual menu of highs and lows for all who watched them. All along the way they played scintillating football and entertained the public. Here are the main memories of a fascinating league season.

AUGUST

For the opening month of a tough campaign, the Gunners remained unbeaten and scored nine goals in just three matches. It could have been quite different had not fate gifted the Gunners a late equaliser at Anfield on the opening weekend. The match had erupted into life either side of the half-time break. First, Joe Cole was shown the red card, giving the Gunners numerical advantage. However, after the break the home side went 1-0 up through David Ngog.

The Gunners worked hard to get back in the game, and in the dying seconds an effort from Marouane Chamakh was scooped into his own goal by Pepe Reina. Arsenal had worked hard for that crucial equaliser - in their next tie the goals came with more ease. Theo Walcott scored his first ever Arsenal hat-trick as the team ran riot against 10-man Blackpool at Emirates Stadium. Joining him on a crowded scoresheet were Arshavin, Diaby and Chamakh.

The month's league commitments were concluded with a trip to Ewood Park. In a rainy lunchtime fixture, Wenger's team played with the assurance of title contenders. Although Blackburn put them under sustained pressure, with Mame Biram Diouf scoring for the home side, it was Arsenal that emerged victorious. Walcott and Arshavin were on-target, with Manuel Almunia in fine fettle at the other end.

15 August Liverpool 1-1 Arsenal (Reina og)

21 August Arsenal 6-0 Blackpool (Walcott 12, 40, 58, Arshavin 32 (pen), Diaby 49, Chamakh 83)

28 August Blackburn Rovers 1-2 Arsenal (Walcott 20, Arshavin 51)

SEPTEMBER

The Gunners were again handed numerical advantage against Bolton Wanderers, after the visitors had Gary Cahill sent off. Wenger's wonderboys had dominated the first-half but it ended all square at 1-1 due to some wasteful finishing from the hosts. In the second-half the Gunners' fire had more aim. On target were Chamakh, Song and Vela. They had taken 10 points from a possible 12 in the season to date.

They were back on the road in the middle of the month, travelling to the north-east to face Sunderland. Captain Fabregas opened the scoring with a lucky goal in the 12th minute. In the second-half, Arsenal were reduced to 10 men when Alex Song was dismissed. The Gunners could have doubled the lead with 17 minutes left, but Tomas Rosicky missed his penalty. How that miss was rued when Darren Bent slotted home a last-minute equaliser for Sunderland, denying Arsenal top spot in the league.

11 September Arsenal 4-1 Bolton Wanderers
(Koscielny 23, Chamakh 60, Song 78, Vela 83)

18 September Sunderland 1-1 Arsenal (Fabregas 12)

25 September Arsenal 2-3 West Bromwich Albion
(Nasri 76, 90)

The team had remained unbeaten for five matches but that run came to an end in unexpected circumstances: at home to West Bromwich Albion. The first-half's most notable action came when Almunia saved a penalty from Chris Brunt. After the break, the Gunners fell behind to two goals in two minutes from the plucky visitors. Jerome Thomas added a third in the 73rd minute. The Gunners threw everything they could at the visitors but could only pull back two goals, both from Nasri.

It was a tough end to the month. Next up in the league was a visit to leaders Chelsea...

Didier Drogba has long been Arsenal's nemesis and the first league match of October proved no exception. He gave Chelsea the lead in the 39th minute and Alex doubled the host's lead in the closing minutes. The 2-0 scoreline did not reflect Arsenal's performance. They put together a series of fine attacks and nearly scored on a number of occasions. Had the line-up not been decimated by suspensions to key players, the outcome could have been quite different.

3 October Chelsea 2-0 Arsenal

16 October Arsenal 2-1 Birmingham City
(Nasri 41 (pen), Chamakh 47)

24 October Manchester City 0-3 Arsenal
(Nasri 20, Song 65, Bendtner 88)

30 October Arsenal 1-0 West Ham United
(Song 88)

Wenger's side needed to bounce back and it did - at Manchester City. The 3-0 win at the City of Manchester Stadium took Arsenal to second place in the Premier League. Nasri, Song and Bendtner were on target. It was Nasri who was most impressive on the day, putting in a fine performance in a season that was becoming increasingly fertile for him. The other notable facts of the match were the appearance of another red card - this time Dedryck Boyata was dismissed for a foul on Marouane Chamakh - and a missed penalty from Fabregas. Most importantly, the Gunners were back in winning ways after the Chelsea setback.

Against West Ham United the Gunners dominated the match but seemed unable to transform their pre-eminence into goals. Robert Green was in great form in the opponent's goal. That, coupled with poor finishing and some even poorer luck, made it seem as if the Gunners would never score.

NOVEMBER

7 November Arsenal 0-1 Newcastle United

10 November Wolverhampton Wanderers 0-2 Arsenal (Chamakh 1, 90)

14 November Everton 1-2 Arsenal (Sagna 35, Fabregas 47)

20 November Arsenal 2-3 Tottenham Hotspur (Nasri 9, Chamakh 27)

27 November Aston Villa 2- 4 Arsenal (Arshavin 38, Nasri 44, Chamakh 55, Wilshere 90)

November turned out to be a classic example of a mixed month for north London's finest. Three wins on the road were welcome, particularly as the team scored eight goals in those three matches. However, two defeats dampened the mood, particularly a spectacular loss against local rivals Tottenham.

The Gunners went into a lunchtime clash with Newcastle United just two points off the top. Andy Carroll's masterful header at the close of the first-half consigned Arsenal to defeat. Three days later Arsenal were back in winning form at Wolves. Marouane Chamakh scored in the first and final minute of a match that Arsenal had dominated.

Strikes from Bacary Sagna and Cesc Fabregas ensured the points for Arsenal at Goodison Park. The rearguard needed to be strong as Everton mounted many counterattacks. Aside from a late consolation strike, the Toffees were held at bay. The travelling Gunners faithful were jubilant at the final whistle.

Against Spurs back at Emirates, Arsenal took a two-goal lead into the half-time break. Just 45 minutes later they had lost to their north London rivals, the first time they had lost to Spurs at home for 17 years. Nasri and Chamakh had afforded Arsenal their half-time lead, but an astonishing second-half comeback from the visitors left Arsenal without the points.

In their next game, at Aston Villa, the Gunners won 4-2. After Arshavin had opened the scoring on 38 minutes and Nasri doubled the lead on the stroke of half-time. In an eventful second period both sides scored twice, and Wilshere's last-gasp goal put the game beyond Villa's reach.

Against Fulham, Arsenal found themselves with the tough task of breaking through a resolutely defensive side. The deadlock was broken on 14 minutes when the superb Nasri left the defenders in his wake to crash home the ball. With 15 minutes of the match remaining Nasri was on target again. In between, it had been hard work for the Gunners, but they finished on top.

Arsenal went into the match at Old Trafford at the top of the Premier League, but United's 1-0 victory in the tie knocked the visitors off their perch. Park's winner, on 40 minutes, was something of a fluke, though United were less fortunate when Wayne Rooney missed a second-half penalty.

After a two-week break over Christmas, the Gunners returned to the fray with the bit between their teeth. Goals from Song, Fabregas and Walcott gave them a victory in an exciting derby against Chelsea. The win put Arsenal back in second place and very much in the title race as the year drew to an end.

The final match of 2010 was at Wigan. Arshavin and Bendtner put Arsenal 2-1 ahead after Wigan's 17th minute opener. However, a late own-goal from Sebastien Squillaci meant the points and the spoils were shared. Thus came to an end an eventful year for Arsenal.

> 4 **December Arsenal 2-1 Fulham** (Nasri 14,75)
> 13 **December Manchester United 1-0 Arsenal**
> 27 **December Arsenal 3-1 Chelsea** (Song 44, Fabregas 50, Walcott 53)
> 29 **December Wigan Athletic 2-2 Arsenal** (Arshavin 38, Bendtner 43)

JAN

1 January Birmingham City 0-3 Arsenal (van Persie 13, Nasri 57, Johnson 65 (og))

5 January Arsenal 0-0 Manchester City

15 January West Ham United 0-3 Arsenal (van Persie 13, 76 (pen), Walcott 41)

22 January Arsenal 3-0 Wigan Athletic (van Persie 21, 59, 85)

The Gunners needed to keep the pressure on their fellow title contenders in January if they were to set up an exciting run-in. They started in perfect style, with a convincing 3-0 win at Birmingham. Van Persie and Nasri scored one each, before a Fabregas drive ricocheted off two Birmingham players and landed in the net. Four days later, Arsenal bossed the match against Manchester City but were unable to turn their pre-eminence into a goal.

Against West Ham in the middle of the month, it was van Persie who epitomised Arsenal's fine victory. He scored twice - including one from the penalty spot - and set up a third for Theo Walcott. January was a busy month for the Gunners, yet they were playing well and already had two 3-0 victories in the Premier League under their belts.

The final league clash of the season ended with the same scoreline in Arsenal's favour. Wigan were the visitors and they must have left wishing they had never set eyes on Robin van Persie. On 85 minutes he completed the first hat-trick of his Arsenal career. He could have had four, but missed a penalty after Fabregas had been fouled. But that did not matter: the hat-trick was his and the win was Arsenal's. The Club had yet to concede a goal in 2011.

FEBRUARY

Louis Saha struck half-way through the first period to give Everton the lead on the first day of the month. After the hour mark, Mr Wenger threw Andrey Arshavin into the fray and he quickly equalised with a fine volley. Just five minutes later, Koscielny netted the winner with a glorious header. As the Gunners celebrated that win, little could they have known what drama would occur during their next tie.

It is rare that a team takes a 4-0 lead into the half-time interval; it is rarer still that a team in that position does not go on to win the match. Arsenal's visit to St James' Park turned into a rare experience indeed. Walcott gave Arsenal the lead in the first minute, and by the half-time whistle Djourou had joined him on the score-sheet, as had Van Persie with a brace. In the second-half Arsenal were reduced to 10 men and fell apart, allowing Newcastle to set up a final scoreline of 4-4.

Next up came Wolves, and after the public reaction to the Newcastle draw the Gunners were keen to put things right, which they did. Van Persie scored in each half. The first saw him convert a Fabregas cross, the second capped a sweeping up-field move involving Walcott and the Spaniard. This was a convincing performance against a Wolves side that had just beaten Manchester United.

The clash with Stoke City was a night of mixed emotions. Sebastien Squillaci's eighth minute header proved the winning goal. However, the sight of Fabregas and Walcott being removed from the match through injury was worrying for all Gunners fans. It had been a tough challenge to overcome the robust and strong Stoke side, but Wenger's young team had managed it.

1 February Arsenal 2-1 Everton
(Arshavin 70, Koscielny 76)

5 February Newcastle United 4-4 Arsenal
(Walcott 1, Djourou 3, van Persie 10, 26)

12 February Arsenal 2-0 Wolverhampton Wanderers (van Persie 16, 56)

23 February Arsenal 1-0 Stoke City
(Squillaci 8)

5 March Arsenal 0-0 Sunderland

19 March West Bromwich Albion 2-2
   Arsenal (Arshavin 70,
   van Persie 77)

With many knock-out tournament commitments in March, the
Gunners were only in action in the Premier League twice. As both
matches ended all-square, Arsenal lost vital ground in the league
just when they could not afford to. Six points in March and they
would have gone into April on top of the league.

A frustrating goalless draw with Sunderland could not have been a
bigger contrast from the 5-0 victory Arsenal had enjoyed in the FA
Cup just days earlier. For the Sunderland tie Wenger made many
changes, and watched his side fruitlessly sweat to overcome
the visitors' superb resistance. Closer and closer came the
Gunners to scoring - but not close enough.

At West Bromwich Albion a fortnight later, Arsenal were
trailing 2-0 with just twenty minutes remaining
on the clock. Defeat here would have been
unthinkable if the Club wanted to stay in the
Premier League hunt. Arshavin scored on
70 minutes and seven minutes later Van
Persie managed to gently stab
the ball over the line. Clichy
came close to managing
a dramatic winner at the
death, but it was not to be.

APRIL

April began as March had ended - with a draw. Blackburn Rovers proved the most impenetrable of opposition, even when reduced to 10 men. Typical of their admirable - if frustrating - defensive strength came at the end of the match when a Bendtner header seemed set to win the game. Michel Salgado cleared the ball off the line just as Gunners fans prepared to celebrate.

Wenger needed his team to return to winning ways. At Blackpool, they did just that. Diaby and Eboue had the Gunners 2-0 up after just 20 minutes. After the hosts pulled a goal back Van Persie put the match beyond doubt with a magnificent volley.

Next up came Spurs, and a chance to avenge November's defeat. A thrilling tie saw the lead swap hands as both teams scored three times. Walcott started the scoring with a breakaway strike on five minutes. After Spurs had equalised, Nasri reclaimed the lead for the visitors with a long-range effort. Van Persie made it 3-1 to Arsenal in the 40th minute. Could victory be looming? Spurs then scored twice to consign another Gunners' league match to finish all-square.

In the wake of that eventful draw, Gunners fans would not have objected to a quiet win. It was 16 matches since they had lost in the Premier League, but too many of those ties had ended in draws. That run came to an end at Bolton, where a last-minute goal from Tamir Cohen condemned Arsenal to a defeat that effectively ended their Premier League title hopes.

 2 April Arsenal 0-0 Blackburn Rovers

10 April Blackpool 1-3 Arsenal
    (Diaby 17, Eboue 20, van Persie 75)

17 April Arsenal 1-1 Liverpool
    (van Persie 90 (pen))

20 April Tottenham Hotspur 3-3 Arsenal
    (Walcott 5, Nasri 12, van Persie 40)

24 April Bolton Wanderers 2-1 Arsenal
    (van Persie 48)

What a way to begin the final month of the campaign: against Manchester United of all teams. United arrived in determined mood, keen to close in on the Premier League title rather than concede ground to Chelsea. Arsenal had other ideas. They dominated the first-half and then, just as United were beginning to wrestle control, Aaron Ramsey scored the winner.

1 May Arsenal 1-0 Manchester United (Ramsey 56)

8 May Stoke City 3-1 Arsenal (van Persie 81)

15 May Arsenal 1-2 Aston Villa (van Persie 89)

22 May Fulham 2-2 Arsenal (van Persie 29, Walcott 89)

Could Arsenal's inconsistent campaign be about to end on a high? Defeat at Stoke extinguished such hope and also mathematically confirmed that the Gunners' season would end trophyless. Van Persie spurned two golden chances before finally scoring with 10 minutes left. By then, Stoke had already done enough to consign their visitors to their seventh defeat of the league campaign.

Aston Villa made it eight defeats when they beat Arsenal 2-1 at Emirates. Again, Van Persie managed a late strike which turned out to be nothing more than a consolation. Darren Bent took advantage of a sluggish start from Arsenal by scoring twice in the opening 15 minutes.

Despite Fulham being reduced to 10 men on the final day, they were all set to beat Arsenal. With their 2-1 lead it seemed the Gunners would lose again. Yet at the death of both the match and the season, Walcott fired past Mark Schwarzer to grab a final point of a frustrating campaign.

BACARY SAGNA

3

The lowdown: Sagna is one of the most reliable players to ever wear an Arsenal shirt. He arrived at the Club in 2007 and was so brilliant from the off that he was voted into the PFA Team of the Season at the end of his debut campaign.

Since then he has been a model of professionalism, brilliance and consistency. Arsenal fans adore him, wingers fear him - he is a magnificent defender. Strong in the tackle and with fine positional awareness, Sagna is not a player often caught unawares by even the most prestigious opposition.

A French international and Premier League star, Sagna is the business!

Bacary says: 'Everybody knows how proud I am to represent Arsenal. Every week we do our best for the Club and its fans. Our team spirit is immense. I believe that very soon we will win the trophies we all wish for.'

Arsène Wenger says:
'We need the very best and Sagna gives us that. He is powerful and quick. His experience and determination are also extremely strong. He is one of the greatest players I have ever managed.'

16

LAURENT KOSCIELNY

6

Name: **Laurent Koscielny**

Born: **September 10, 1985 Tulle, France**

Squad Number: **6**

Position: **Defender**

Previous Clubs: **En Avant Guingamp Tours, Lorient**

Joined Gunners: **July 07, 2010**

In his debut campaign for the Gunners, Laurent was a towering figure in defence. Already he is being mentioned as a Club legend.

The lowdown: Laurent enjoyed a speedy rise in French football. He was voted Best Player in Ligue 2 by fellow professionals at the end of the 2008/09 season and then moved to the top-flight club Lorient. He thrived there and after just one season was snapped up by Arsène Wenger.

He is fast of mind and body which helps his combination of defensive brilliance and creative, attacking venture. He scored his first goal for Arsenal in September, against Bolton Wanderers. He is a combative defender and has occasionally faced the wrath of referees. However, he is a true professional and a firm favourite of the Gunners faithful.

Laurent says: 'I am playing at my best. I am more confident and I have realised that I have the ability to become a regular player here and do well for this club. I am also very grateful to the fans who have always supported me since joining the Club. Their support was a big help for me.'

Arsène Wenger says: 'We identified Koscielny as a very, very strong centre half. He is an outstanding addition to our team. He settled quickly and improved throughout the season. He controls the game and thinks quickly.'

Champions League

Arsenal v Braga

Braga were the Gunners' first European opponents of the season. They were brushed aside 6-0, with a fine Marouane Chamakh taking the pick of the goals. It was made possible by a mischievous back-heel pass from Jack Wilshere. Fabregas and Vela both scored twice on a rampant evening at Emirates.

Euro fact: Braga went on to become the Europa League finalists.

Partisan Belgrade v Arsenal

In a superb away performance, the Gunners won 3-1 in their second tie of the campaign. Wilshere set up Arshavin's opener in the 15th minute. Then, second-half headers from Chamakh and Squillaci sealed the win.

Euro fact: There were three penalty kicks in this tie.

Arsenal v Shakhtar Donetsk

By the end of this entertaining tie the Gunners were in an invincible position in the competition: played three, won three, scored 14. Alex Song, Samir Nasri, Cesc Fabregas, Jack Wilshere and Marouane Chamakh were the scorers in this pulsating match. The game was also memorable for the presence of former Gunner Eduardo in the visitors' ranks.

Shakhtar Donetsk v Arsenal

In the ninth minute, Theo Walcott capped a fine breakaway with a goal. However, this early lead was not to result in a repeat of the romp Arsenal had enjoyed in the previous tie. An own goal from Craig Eastmond and a strike from Eduardo consigned Arsenal to their first defeat of the campaign. The home side had been powerful on the break all night.

Braga v Arsenal

Having started so promisingly, Arsenal were by now losing ground in the Group. They lost 2-0 against Braga, with both goals coming from Matheus in the final seven minutes. The Gunners had attempted to score all night, with Kieran Gibbs their most potent threat. This defeat put extra pressure on their final Group H tie.

Euro fact:
This was the 11th successive season that the Gunners reached the last 16 of the competition.

Arsenal v Partizan Belgrade

A victory was essential in this tie and Arsenal got one thanks to strikes from Van Persie, Walcott and Nasri. The Dutchman netted from the penalty spot, but it was only when the next two strikes were fired home in the 73rd and 77th minutes that the Gunners could begin to breathe easily. Cleo had equalised in between, piling the pressure on Arsenal. All ended well, with the Gunners qualifying for the knock-out stages.

Euro fact: The Gunners ended the match with 10 men: Eboue became injured after Wenger had used all his substitutes.

15 September
Arsenal 6-0 Braga (Fabregas (2), Arshavin , Chamakh , Vela (2))

28 September
Arsenal 3-1 Partizan Belgrade (Arshavin, Chamakh, Squillaci)

19 October
Arsenal 5-1 Shaktar Donestk (Song, Nasri , Fabregas (pen), Wilshere Chamakh)

3 November
Shaktar Donetsk 2-1 Arsenal (Walcott)

23 November 2010 – Braga 2-0 Arsenal

8 December 2010
Arsenal 3-1 Partizan Belgrade (Van Persie, Walcott, Nasri)

Knockout Stage

Arsenal v Barcelona

If any Gunners fans were nervous about the team's prospects against Spanish giants Barcelona, they were reassured by this famous victory. After Villa had given Barca the lead on 26 minutes, many commentators expected the visitors to claim victory. However, 12 minutes from the end, Van Persie fired home a cracker from a tight angle. Then, five minutes later, Nasri set up the winner for Arshavin. The Gunners fans leapt with joy, and waved the flags that the Club had put under every seat.

Barcelona v Arsenal

Three weeks on from the Emirates victory, the Gunners faced Barca for the second-leg at the Nou Camp. It was a night of tension, controversy and heartbreak. Messi opened the scoring after a rare Fabregas mistake, but Arsenal drew level seven minutes later thanks to a Barca own goal. Xavi put the home side back in front and - following the contentious dismissal of Van Persie - Messi capped the victory from the penalty spot.

16 February 2011
Arsenal 2-1 Barcelona
(Van Persie, Arshavin)

8 March 2011
Barcelona 3-1 Arsenal
(Busquets (og))

The Men of the Match

Here are five stand-out player performances from the 2010/11 campaign. Football is a team game, but sometimes one individual stands out over 90 minutes.

Arsenal 5-1 Shakhtar Donetsk

Man of the Match: Jack Wilshere

In this glorious five-goal performance from the Gunners, they truly declared their ambition for the UEFA Champions League. They were in it to win it! The finest player on the night was 19-year-old Jack Wilshere. The English midfielder was at the heart of the Arsenal attacks and also helped marshal the midfield's defensive duties. In the 66th minute, he scored. He raced onto Chamakh's touch, swapped passes with Rosicky and lifted a shot over the advancing goalkeeper.

Arsenal 3-1 Chelsea

Man of the match: Theo Walcott

It was three frantic second-half minutes that settled this tie for the Gunners. During them, Walcott and Fabregas each scored and set up a goal each. The first came when Walcott drew Cech and tapped the ball to the captain to score. Then, Fabregas and Walcott played a one-two which ended with the young Englishman scoring his ninth goal in eight appearances. Walcott had been majestic throughout the match and deserved his man-of-the match status.

Arsenal 6-0 Braga

Man of the match: Cesc Fabregas

In the ninth minute of this UEFA Champions League tie, captain Fabregas opened the scoring from the penalty spot. The home fans erupted with joy, little knowing how much excitement was to come. At the centre of that excitement was Fabregas. He also set-up two more goals - for Arshavin and Vela - as well as netting again himself, with a fine header. Only a goal-line clearance prevented him from completing his first hat-trick.

Arsenal 5-0 Leyton Orient

Man of the match: Nicklas Bendtner

By the 62nd minute of this cup derby, the Danish striker was celebrating his second hat-trick for the Club having fired his third goal of the game from the penalty spot. On the half-hour, he had opened his account for the match, heading home a cross from Kieran Gibbs. Some 13 minutes later he received the ball from Rosicky, cut inside and blasted a cross-shot home. Then came his second-half penalty to complete the hat-trick.

Arsenal 1-0 Manchester United

Man of the match: Aaron Ramsey

Just as Manchester United were beginning to take command of this engaging late-season Premier League tie, the young Welshman Ramsey stepped up and smashed in the winning goal for the Gunners. He had been a late addition to the side after Fabregas was ruled out with injury at the last moment. This was only Ramsey's second start since he had broken his leg the previous year. But his match-winning performance belied this fact.

The Wonder of Wenger

A virtual unknown among football fans here when he arrived at Arsenal in 1996, Mr Wenger is now one of the most successful and celebrated managers in English football history. Here, we pay tribute to the Frenchman and list just some of his many magnificent achievements and qualities.

FACT
He is the only Gunners manager to have won the FA Cup more than once and the only manager to take the Club to a Champions League Final.

FACT
He was also the first manager in English league history to complete an entire 38-game season unbeaten in 2003/04.

FACT
Arsène holds an economics degree from Strasbourg University and has also been awarded an honorary DSc by the University of Hertfordshire.

FACT
He has received numerous personal awards and honours, including an OBE and France's highest honour, Légion d'Honneur. He has been inducted into the English football Hall of Fame and has even had an asteroid named after him!

The Manager played a crucial role in planning and designing Emirates Stadium, including the size of the pitch and the design and temperature of the dressing rooms.

He also arranged for the temperature on the team bus to be adjusted in order to keep the muscles of the Arsenal team as supple as possible. Mr Wenger was closely involved in the design of the new Training Centre - he even chose the furniture and the cutlery!

He was named 'Manager of the Year' in 1998, 2002 and 2004.

The Club commissioned a bronze bust of Wenger to be made. This was the first time an Arsenal Manager had been honoured since Herbert Chapman way back in the 1930s!

The biggest home wins under Wenger were the 7-0 victories against Slavia Prague (2007), Middlesbrough (2006) and Everton (2005).

The biggest away win of his reign to date was at Middlesbrough in 1999. The Gunners won 6-1.

No Gunners Manager has presided over more matches than Mr Wenger.

He was awarded the Freedom of Islington in 2004.

The Frenchman is fluent in five languages.

Trophies won under Wenger:

Premier League champions:
1998, 2002, 2004

FA Cup winners:
1998, 2002, 2003, 2005

Charity/Community Shield winners
1998, 1999, 2002, 2004

The FA Cup

3rd Round

Home v Leeds United

For the majority of the second-half of the Club's opening FA Cup tie of the campaign, it seemed as if a major cup shock was on the cards. Robert Snodgrass scored from the spot for Leeds in the 54th minute, his side were set to be the first lower league team for 15 years to knock the Gunners out of the famous competition. Then in the final minute, with the Leeds fans preparing to celebrate such an occurrence, Theo Walcott won a penalty for Arsenal, which Fabregas converted.

Away v Leeds United

At Elland Road, Wenger's team dominated the replay and won comfortably. Nasri gave them the lead on five minutes and by the final whistle, Sagna and Van Persie had joined him on the scoresheet. The Dutchman's strike was the pick of the evening: he headed home a Bendtner cross and celebrated by sliding onto his front. He nearly added another during the closing moments of this superb win.

MATCH FACT

Mr Wenger made nine changes to the line-up compared with the Club's previous match.

MATCH FACT

Leeds goalkeeper, Kasper Schmeichel, is the son of legendary Manchester United keeper Peter Schmeichel.

4th Round
Home v Huddersfield Town

For the second tie running, a late spot-kick from captain Cesc Fabregas saved the Gunners' blushes against lower league opposition. A deflected first-half drive from Bendtner had given the home team the lead, but the scores were levelled by Alan Lee in the 66th minute. Four minutes from time Bendtner won a penalty for Arsenal which Spaniard Fabregas drove home to send the Gunners through to the next round.

5th round
Away v Leyton Orient

Against the east London minnows, there was once more a crucial late goal. However, this time the goal was scored by their opponents. Eight minutes into the second-half, Tomas Rosicky gave the Gunners a deserved lead with a thumping header. Orient upped their game in response and attacked ferociously. Arsenal attempted to capitalise on this via counter attacks but were unable to double their fragile lead. With just two minutes remaining, substitute Jonathan Tehoue levelled the score and sent the tie to a surprising replay.

The FA Cup

Home v Leyton Orient

In the replay at Emirates Stadium, the Gunners showed their superior class with a memorable 5-0 triumph. Goals from Chamakh and Clichy opened and closed the scoring. In-between, Bendtner had fired a sensational hat-trick, his second for the Club. This was more like it. On a cold winter night the Arsenal supporters were warmed by the sight of their team in such superior flowing form. Could they be watching a cup-winning side, they dared to wonder.

MATCH FACT

Clichy's 75th-minute goal was only his second in 255 appearances for Arsenal.

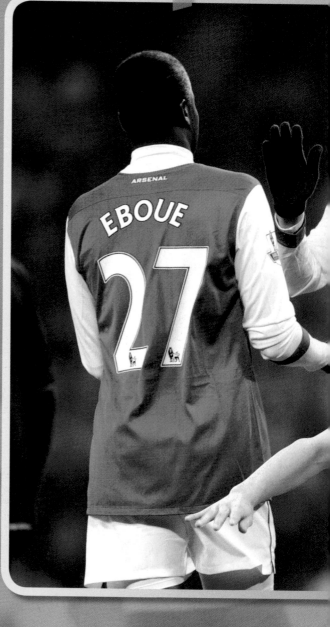

Away v Manchester United

How did Arsenal lose this Saturday evening tie at Old Trafford? They were in domineering form, enjoying the majority of possession and unleashing the majority of the game's shots on goal. However, when it really mattered it was United who made the difference with a goal in each half. The first game from Fabio, the second from Rooney. These strikes brought to an end an eventful FA Cup campaign for the Gunners.

RESULTS

8 January 2011:
Arsenal 1-1 Leeds United
(Fabregas (pen), 90)

19 January 2011:
Leeds United 1-3 Arsenal
(Nasri 5, Sagna 34, van Persie 76)

30 January 2011:
Arsenal 2-1 Huddersfield Town
(Bendtner 21, Fabregas (pen) 86)

20 February 2011:
Leyton Orient 1-1 Arsenal
(Rosicky 53)

2 March 2011:
Arsenal 5-0 Leyton Orient
(Chamakh 7, Bendtner 30, 43, 62 (pen), Clichy 75)

12 March 2011:

Manchester United 2-0 Arsenal

MATCH FACT
The tie saw the return of Aaron Ramsey, following a lengthy absence due to a broken leg.

125 in the Making

Arsenal Football Club celebrates its 125th anniversary during the 2011/12 season. Among the initiatives to mark this is a new shirt, which features a special 125th anniversary crest design combining the graphic of the first Club crest with the current version. Here, we recall the key milestones in the Club's 125 years to date.

1886: Royal Arsenal was formed in Woolwich.

1891: The Club turns professional and changes its name to Woolwich Arsenal.

1893: The first league game, against Newcastle United in September. It ended in a 2-2 draw. Later that year, the team beat Ashford United 12-0 in the FA Cup.

1913: The Club changes its name to Arsenal (though many referred to it informally as 'The Arsenal'). In September, the first match at Arsenal Stadium, Highbury is played.

1915: Arsenal, despite finishing fifth in the Second Division, are promoted to the First. They have remained there ever since.

1925: Herbert Chapman is appointed Arsenal Manager. He said it would take five years to build a trophy-winning team.

1930: The Manager's prophecy was proved correct when the Club won its first major trophy, the FA Cup.

1931: The first league title is secured.

1934: Arsenal provide seven of England's starting XI for a friendly against world champions Italy, a record contribution which stands to this day.

1935: The Gunners win their third league title after a magnificent campaign. Leicester and Middlesbrough had been beaten 8-0, Liverpool were thrashed 8-1 and Wolves were walloped 7-0. There was also a 6-0 win at Tottenham to provide the icing on the cake.

1927

1936

1936: The Stadium's art-deco East Stand was officially opened.

1948: Arsenal won the league by seven points.

1950: The Club wins another FA Cup

1966: The youth team win the FA Youth Cup - could this be a sign of something special to come?

1971: After a glorious season, the Gunners were double-winners.

1971

1950

125 in the Making

1979: Arsenal win the FA Cup, beating Manchester United 3-0 after a stunning match. They were runners-up in the competition in the years either side of this win.

1987: New Manager George Graham guides the Club to victory in the League Cup. They beat Liverpool 2-1.

1989: The Gunners win silverware against Liverpool again: this time winning the league title in a thrilling encounter at Anfield.

1979

1987

1993: Having won another title in 1991, Graham's team makes history by becoming the first to win both the FA Cup and League Cup in one season.

1994: Parma are beaten 1-0 in a tense European Cup Winners' Cup Final.

1998: French Manager Arsène Wenger leads a dynamic team to the league and cup double.

1993

2002

2002: The second double of the Frenchman's reign is sealed with a 1-0 victory at Old Trafford.

2004: Another Premiership title is won, in a season that saw the Gunners unbeaten in the league. They then overturned Nottingham Forest's long-standing record of league games without defeat. Played 49, Won 36, Drawn 13, Lost None

2006: The Club reach the UEFA Champions League Final and move from Highbury to their new home: Emirates Stadium.

2011: Arsenal celebrates its 125th anniversary.

2011

Jack Wilshere 19

Name: Jack Wilshere

Born: January 01, 1992, Stevenage, Hertfordshire

Squad Number: 19

Position: Midfielder

Previous Club: Bolton (loan)

Joined Gunners: October 01, 2001

When Jack Wilshere joined the Club as a nine year-old boy, few could have hoped he would enjoy such a spectacular rise to become one of European football's most admired teenage talents. By the time he was 16 years of age he had become a revered member of the Reserve team.

He made his first-team debut against Blackburn in 2008 aged 16 years and 256 days. He was also the youngest Arsenal player to appear in European football when he came on against Dynamo Kiev on November 25, 2008 aged 16 years and 329 days

He was sent for a loan spell at Bolton Wanderers where he further honed his abilities and grabbed crucial experience. He returned to the Gunners an ever more formidable midfield talent. Jack is creative, strong, intelligent and versatile. He is also now a key part of the England team, having made his debut on the same night as fellow Gunner Kieran Gibbs.

Jack says: 'I just have to thank the boss for that really. He put me in the team for the first game against Liverpool and stuck with me ever since really. Hopefully I have done enough to keep my place, and paid the manager back.'

Arsène Wenger says:
'It has been an excellent season where he delivered beyond expectation. He has had a formidable presence in midfield with a lot of character, he is a fighter, a great passer of the ball. He has played a lot. He deserves it.'

34

Kieran Gibbs
28

Name: Kieran Gibbs

Born: September 26, 1989
Lambeth, London

Position: Defender/Midfielder

Squad Number: 28

Previous Club: Norwich City
(Loan), Wimbledon

Joined Gunners:
September 10, 2007

Kieran came through the Arsenal Academy as a wide midfielder, having previously come through the Wimbledon Academy which was disbanded when the club relocated to Milton Keynes. He made his first-team debut in the same match as Jack Wilshere.

The youngster is a fast, intelligent player with wonderful technique and awareness. He is also a versatile player as he showed when he made his senior England debut at left-back. Indeed, it was Mr Wenger who spotted Gibbs' potential as a left-back after a successful loan spell with Norwich City.

With his natural attacking instincts, Kieran is an exciting player wherever he plays. Having put an unfortunate injury behind him, he is set to become a major star for Club and country. Watch out for him!

Kieran says: 'My team-mates were fantastic when I was been in the treatment room. Now I want to put that behind me and give my all for Arsenal Football Club. I'm very excited for the future.'

Arsène Wenger says:
'He can play left midfield or he can play left back. His ability and maturity are immense. He is also a focused professional. I believe he is a bright and valuable prospect for both Arsenal and England. This campaign could really make him.'

The Carling Cup

Tottenham Hotspur v Arsenal

The Gunners kicked off the Carling Cup campaign with a visit to their local rivals. 120 minutes and five goals later, they were in the hat for the next round. As the tie had moved into extra time, the teams were stuck at 1-1, but then three goals handed victory to Arsenal. The breathless clash saw goals from Lansbury, Arshavin and a brace of penalties from Nasri. At the end, the visiting fans taunted their rivals by chanting: 'Shall we make a DVD?' There are few better ways to start a cup campaign than by knocking out Spurs.

Newcastle United v Arsenal

On the stroke of half-time, Newcastle goalkeeper scored an own-goal. In a pulsating second-half, Arsenal added three more goals to the scoreline. The first was a cool finish from Walcott in the 53rd minute. Bendtner then made it three before Walcott capped a much deserved victory by scoring after soaring free of the defence. Arsenal were 4-0 winners and this win left them just two steps from a long overdue return to Wembley Stadium.

Arsenal v Wigan Athletic

Arsenal reached the League Cup Semi-Final for a record 14th time with a 2-0 win over Wigan on a snowy evening in North London. Four minutes from the end of the first period, Antolin Alcaraz inadvertently nodded a Theo Walcott corner past his own goalkeeper. In the second-half, Nicklas Bendtner slid in a useful cross from Carlos Vela to make it 2-0. The Gunners could have scored twice more in the closing stages, but the two-goal lead was enough to send them through to the next round. Could silverware be on the cards?

Ipswich Town v Arsenal

Ipswich Town earned a surprise victory in the Semi-Final first leg with a breakaway strike from Tamas Priskin. His goal came just 12 minutes from time and Arsenal were unable to peg the hosts back. Indeed, in the dying minutes the Gunners very nearly conceded again. Before which, Fabregas and Walcott had come close to scoring - but not close enough. Arsenal would have a challenge on their hands in the semi-final stay involved.

Arsenal v Ipswich Town

A wondrous goal from Nicklas Bendtner broke the visitor's brave resistance in the 61st minute of the second-leg. Laurent Koscielny's header then gave Arsenal a belated lead in the tie. With 13 minutes left, Andrey Arshavin set up Cesc Fabregas for a third. At the back, the Gunners kept it tight, with Johan Djourou in marshalling mood in this, his 100th appearance for the Club. When the final whistle sounded the Gunners were ecstatic: the Club had reached its seventh League Cup Final. There, they would face Birmingham City.

Arsenal v Birmingham City

This was a bitter defeat for the Gunners fans at Wembley and watching from home around the world. Zigic's opener for City was cancelled out on 38 minutes by Van Persie's momentous volley. The match seemed destined for extra-time, but then fate intervened. In the final minute, Ben Foster fired in a free-kick which was flicked on by Nikola Zigic. Wojciech Szczesny was distracted and could only fumble the ball into the path of Obafemi Martins, who gleefully scored the winner.

21 September
Tottenham Hotspur 1-4 Arsenal
(Lansbury 15, Nasri 91 (pen),
95 (pen), Arshavin 105)

27 October
Newcastle United 0-4 Arsenal
(Krul 45 (og), Walcott 53, 88,
Bendtner 82)

30 November
Arsenal 2-0 Wigan Athletic
(Alcaraz 41 (og), Bendtner 67)

12 January
Ipswich Town 1-0 Arsenal

25 January
Arsenal 3-0 Ipswich Town
(Bendtner 61, Koscielny 64,
Fabregas 77)

27 February
Arsenal 1-2 Birmingham City
(van Persie 38)

New Faces

Arsenal Football Club added some fresh names to its squad during the summer. Here is the lowdown on some of the new faces that will be delighting fans in the future.

Ryo Miyaichi

The young Japanese striker is an exciting prospect. He impressed during a trial in the summer of 2010 when he featured in pre-season friendlies against Boreham Wood and AFC Wimbledon. He can play as a centre-forward or on the left or right wing.

Such versatility makes him a vital option for the Club during the lengthy and busy campaigns Arsenal participate in. Having spent time on-loan at Feyenoord he has additional experience which will be of use to both him and his team-mates. With his work permit granted he is ready for action.

Arsène Wenger said: 'He trialled with us last summer and has raw ability which has attracted many clubs around the world.'

Name: Ryo Miyaichi
Born: December 14, 1992
Squad Number: 31
Position: Striker
Previous Club: Feyenoord (loan)
Joined Gunners: January, 2011

Gervinho

Name: Gervinho
Born: May 27,1987, Anyama, Ivory Coast
Squad Number: 27
Position: Striker
Previous Club: Beveren, Le Mans, Lille
Joined Gunners: July 18, 2011

Gervinho joined the Club after a vintage campaign in France. During the 2010/11 season, The Ivorian scored 18 goals in 49 matches for Lille as the club won the Ligue 1 and Coupe de France double. It was his second season for Lille, following two years with another Ligue 1 side, Le Mans.

He is an accomplished striker on the international stage. He represented the Ivory Coast at the 2010 World Cup in South Africa having scored crucial goals during the qualification matches. At the Olympics in Beijing in 2008, he had proudly worn the captain's armband.

Joel Campbell

Young Joel is a striker who has already made a big name for himself in European football thanks to his precocious talent. He has two seasons under his belt in the Primera División, where he turned out for Deportivo Saprissa and also on loan at Puntarenas, making a total of eight league appearances.

Name: Joel Campbell

Born: June 26, 1992, San Jose, Costa Rica

Position: Striker

Previous Club: Deportivo Saprissa, Puntarenas (loan)

Joined Gunners: August 12, 2011

The teenager is already a promising figure on the international arena, having been named in the Costa Rica squad for the 2011 Copa America and the Under-20 World Cup. He is a speedy and composed, predominantly left-footed attacker with impressive instincts and skill.

Arsène Wenger said: "Joel Campbell has already shown that he is a player with great ability, and has also performed well on the international stage at a young age."

Alex Oxlade-Chamberlain

Alex is an exciting and versatile player who can speed down the wing and also operate as a creative spark in the middle of the field. He had joined the Southampton Academy as a seven-year-old and quickly captured the attention of the coaching staff. He made his first-team debut at the tender age of 16 years and 199 days.

Name: Alex Oxlade-Chamberlain

Born: August 15, 1993, Portsmouth

Squad Number: 15

Position: Striker

Previous Club: Southhampton

Joined Gunners: August 8, 2011

He made 44 full appearances for Southampton before moving to the Gunners. He had been a target for several top clubs when he signed for the Club. Arsenal had been tracking him for some time and the Club is delighted to have the services of a player who could be one of the brightest English talents in the future.

Arsène Wenger said: "We are delighted that Alex has decided to join us. He is an exciting young player who will provide us with creativity and offensive quality. Alex is a perceptive passer of the ball and has a great understanding of the game and looks to be a very good team player."

HOME IS WHERE THE

An appreciation of Emirates Stadium

Officially opened by HRH Duke of Edinburgh, Prince Philip, on October 26 2006, Emirates Stadium is the home of The Arsenal Football Club. It is the third-biggest football stadium in England, and holds international matches and rock concerts. An average of 1,140,000 supporters visit the Stadium every season. For Gunners fans, there really is no place like home.

Capacity 60,000 people

First match at Emirates Stadium
v Ajax July 22 2006
(the Dennis Bergkamp Testimonial)
Arsenal 2 - 1 Ajax
(Henry 55, Kanu 80)

First competitive match
v Aston Villa August 19 2006.
Arsenal 1 (Gilberto 83) Aston Villa (Mellberg 54)

First Arsenal goal
Gilberto v Aston Villa August 19 2006

First hat-trick
Jay Simpson v Cardiff City February 19 2007
(FA Youth Cup)

Highest attendance
Premiership 60,161 v Manchester United
November 3 2007

Biggest home wins in 2010/11
6-0 vs Blackpool (August 21) and Braga
(September 15)

Past homes

Stadium fact

The 100 flights of stairs in the Stadium, if combined in height, would be twice as high as Canary Wharf tower!

Stadium fact

The pitch is 113 by 76 metres

Stadium fact

The first eight Premier League matches at Emirates Stadium ended either 3-0 or 1-1.

Stadium fact

The first and 50th competitive matches at Emirates Stadium were both against Aston Villa and both finished with a 1-1 draw.

The Manor Ground

This was the home of the Club for two periods: between 1888 and 1890, and 1893 and 1913. Here, the large steeply-banked terrace became known as Spion Kop, a name given by soldiers returning from the Boer war.

Invicta Ground

In between the two stays at the Manor Ground, the Club played at the Invicta in Plumstead, South-East London. This venue was just a short walk from the Manor Ground, and it was here that the Club began to attract bigger and bigger attendances.

Arsenal Stadium (aka Highbury)

Although nearly always referred to as 'Highbury', the correct title of the Gunners' home between 1913 and 2007 was actually 'Arsenal Stadium'. Arsenal paid £20,000 for an initial 21-year lease on the six acres of land the ground was built on. The first match was a 2-1 victory over Leicester Fosse. In the final match at the stadium, Thierry Henry scored a hat-trick as Arsenal beat Wigan Athletic 4-2 to secure a UEFA Champions League spot, at the expense of local rivals Tottenham Hotspur.

Crossword

Think your Arsenal knowledge is pretty good? Test your knowledge in the crossword below, then check your answers on page 61.

ACROSS

1   He skippered the Gunners during 2010/11 (8)

4   Which Spanish team did Arsenal beat in the UEFA Champions League at Emirates? (9)

7   Where the Club lives (8)

8   Ooh, to be a _____ (6)

11 The Gunners' young English midfielder is Jack _____ (8)

12 The Manager of Arsenal Football Club (6)

14 The 'man in black' at each match (8)

16 He stands guard between the sticks (10)

DOWN

2   The Gunners beat _____ 6-0 in their first Premier League win of 2010/11 (9)

3   The German who came back (7)

5   What league do the Gunners play in? (7)

6   Also known as 'the onion bag' (3)

9   The name the Club's previous home was known by (8)

10 The name of the team we all love (7)

13 Come on you ____ (4)

15 ____ Walcott, scores for Arsenal (4)

Spot the Ball

Use your skill and judgement to see if you can spot the real match ball from the fake ones we've put in, then check your answers on page 61.

The Season in Quotes

Football is a game of opinions and every season is packed with verdicts, thoughts and other pronouncements. These words sum up the dramatic highs and lows of the game as well as statistics do. So here is the story of the 2010/11 campaign through the words of the players and Manager of Arsenal Football Club.

'When he has got the ball he is very calm, that's something that sometimes younger guys don't have – they panic a little bit or something. With him you don't see that though – he is very comfortable with the ball.' - Tomas Rosicky praises Jack Wilshere's man-of-the-match performance in the Carling Cup victory over Spurs.

'We won't get ahead of ourselves with this result' - Theo Walcott after his man-of-the-match performance in the 6-0 thumping of Blackpool.

'I think the number of goals we are scoring shows that Arsenal are ready to go as far as possible in the Champions League' - Johan Djourou, following the 5-1 victory over Shakhtar Donetsk.

'You could sense the atmosphere. The fans were right up for it, just like the players were and we just didn't let Chelsea play.' - Theo Walcott in jubilant mood after the 3-1 win over Chelsea.

'Arsenal has a goalkeeper emergency. I'll happily step into the breach.' German goalkeeping ace Jens Lehmann on his return to the Club in March.

Manager's Comments

'I knew at 4-0 the game was not over because it was important to keep our nerves and continue to play. A team that has already lost the game, when they get back into the game you are always under threat.' Mr Wenger on the dramatic 4-4 draw with Newcastle United

'The team has accumulated a lot of experience despite their age. They are 23 on average but football-wise they are 26 or 27. I gave them a chance to play at a young age and I don't regret that.'

'If I could give any advice to young players now it would be to listen to what people tell you, and live your life off the pitch how you do on it – always be professional and live your life as a footballer.' on lessons learned during 2010/11.

'To score against Barcelona for any player is a very crucial moment, maybe in your career' Andrey Arshavin on his winner against the Spanish giants.

'Robin is a very important player for us, he is the perfect striker, he can do everything and understands the game very, very well.' - Cesc Fabregas on top scorer Van Persie.

The Season in Stats
2010 – 2011

MANUEL ALMUNIA

Prem Lge		Europe		FA Cup		Lge Cup		C. Shield		Total	
Ap	Gl	Ap	Gl	Ap	Gl	Ap	Gl	Ap	Gl	Ap	Gl
8	0	1+1	0	4	0	0	0	0	0	13+1	0

ABOU DIABY

Prem Lge		Europe		FA Cup		Lge Cup		C. Shield		Total	
Ap	Gl	Ap	Gl	Ap	Gl	Ap	Gl	Ap	Gl	Ap	Gl
13+3	2	1	0	3	0	0	0	0	0	17+3	2

BACARY SAGNA

Prem Lge		Europe		FA Cup		Lge Cup		C. Shield		Total	
Ap	Gl	Ap	Gl	Ap	Gl	Ap	Gl	Ap	Gl	Ap	Gl
33	1	4	0	3	1	2+1	0	0	0	42+1	2

CESC FABREGAS

Prem Lge		Europe		FA Cup		Lge Cup		C. Shield		Total	
Ap	Gl	Ap	Gl	Ap	Gl	Ap	Gl	Ap	Gl	Ap	Gl
22+3	3	5	3	0+3	2	2+1	1	0	0	29+7	9

THOMAS VERMAELEN

Prem Lge		Europe		FA Cup		Lge Cup		C. Shield		Total	
Ap	Gl	Ap	Gl	Ap	Gl	Ap	Gl	Ap	Gl	Ap	Gl
5	0	0	0	0	0	0	0	0	0	5	0

LAURENT KOSCIELNY

Prem Lge		Europe		FA Cup		Lge Cup		C. Shield		Total	
Ap	Gl	Ap	Gl	Ap	Gl	Ap	Gl	Ap	Gl	Ap	Gl
30	2	4	0	3	0	6	1	0	0	43	3

TOMAS ROSICKYA

Prem Lge		Europe		FA Cup		Lge Cup		C. Shield		Total	
Ap	Gl	Ap	Gl	Ap	Gl	Ap	Gl	Ap	Gl	Ap	Gl
8+13	0	5	0	3+2	1	3	0	0	0	19+15	1

SAMIR NASRI

Prem Lge		Europe		FA Cup		Lge Cup		C. Shield		Total	
Ap	Gl	Ap	Gl	Ap	Gl	Ap	Gl	Ap	Gl	Ap	Gl
28+2	10	6+2	2	3+1	1	2+2	2	0	0	39+7	15

ROBIN VAN PERSIE

Prem Lge		Europe		FA Cup		Lge Cup		C. Shield		Total	
Ap	Gl	Ap	Gl	Ap	Gl	Ap	Gl	Ap	Gl	Ap	Gl
19+6	18	3	2	1+1	1	3	1	0	0	26+7	22

JENS LEHMANN

Prem Lge		Europe		FA Cup		Lge Cup		C. Shield		Total	
Ap	Gl	Ap	Gl	Ap	Gl	Ap	Gl	Ap	Gl	Ap	Gl
1	0	0	0	0	0	0	0	0	0	1	0

THEO WALCOTT

Prem Lge		Europe		FA Cup		Lge Cup		C. Shield		Total	
Ap	Gl	Ap	Gl	Ap	Gl	Ap	Gl	Ap	Gl	Ap	Gl
19+9	9	3+2	2	0+1	0	3+1	2	0	0	25-13	13

DENILSON

Prem Lge		Europe		FA Cup		Lge Cup		C. Shield		Total	
Ap	Gl	Ap	Gl	Ap	Gl	Ap	Gl	Ap	Gl	Ap	Gl
6+10	0	3+2	0	6	0	5	0	0	0	20+12	0

AARON RAMSEY

Prem Lge		Europe		FA Cup		Lge Cup		C. Shield		Total	
Ap	Gl	Ap	Gl	Ap	Gl	Ap	Gl	Ap	Gl	Ap	Gl
5+2	1	0	0	0+1	0	0	0	0	0	5+3	1

ALEX SONG

Prem Lge		Europe		FA Cup		Lge Cup		C. Shield		Total	
Ap	Gl	Ap	Gl	Ap	Gl	Ap	Gl	Ap	Gl	Ap	Gl
30+1	4	5	1	3+1	0	1+1	0	0	0	39+3	5

SEBASTIEN SQUILLACI

Prem Lge		Europe		FA Cup		Lge Cup		C. Shield		Total	
Ap	Gl	Ap	Gl	Ap	Gl	Ap	Gl	Ap	Gl	Ap	Gl
20+2	1	6	1	4	0	0	0	0	0	30+2	2

CARLOS VELA

Prem Lge		Europe		FA Cup		Lge Cup		C. Shield		Total	
Ap	Gl	Ap	Gl	Ap	Gl	Ap	Gl	Ap	Gl	Ap	Gl
0+4	1	0+4	2	0+1	0	3+1	0	0	0	3+10	3

JACK WILSHERE

Prem Lge		Europe		FA Cup		Lge Cup		C. Shield		Total	
Ap	Gl	Ap	Gl	Ap	Gl	Ap	Gl	Ap	Gl	Ap	Gl
31+4	1	7	1	1+1	0	5	0	0	0	44+5	2

JOHAN DJOUROU

Prem Lge		Europe		FA Cup		Lge Cup		C. Shield		Total	
Ap	Gl	Ap	Gl	Ap	Gl	Ap	Gl	Ap	Gl	Ap	Gl
20+2	1	6	0	3	0	6	0	0	0	35+2	1

LUKASZ FABIANSKI

Prem Lge		Europe		FA Cup		Lge Cup		C. Shield		Total	
Ap	Gl	Ap	Gl	Ap	Gl	Ap	Gl	Ap	Gl	Ap	Gl
14	0	5	0	0	0	1	0	0	0	20	0

ANDREY ARSHAVIN

Prem Lge		Europe		FA Cup		Lge Cup		C. Shield		Total	
Ap	Gl	Ap	Gl	Ap	Gl	Ap	Gl	Ap	Gl	Ap	Gl
25+12	6	3+3	3	5	0	3+1	1	0	0	36+16	10

EMMANUEL EBOUE

Prem Lge		Europe		FA Cup		Lge Cup		C. Shield		Total	
Ap	Gl	Ap	Gl	Ap	Gl	Ap	Gl	Ap	Gl	Ap	Gl
8+5	1	4+2	0	3	0	4+1	0	0	0	19+8	1

KIERAN GIBBS

Prem Lge		Europe		FA Cup		Lge Cup		C. Shield		Total	
Ap	Gl	Ap	Gl	Ap	Gl	Ap	Gl	Ap	Gl	Ap	Gl
4+3	0	3	0	6	0	4	0	0	0	17+3	0

MAROUANE CHAMAKH

Prem Lge		Europe		FA Cup		Lge Cup		C. Shield		Total	
Ap	Gl	Ap	Gl	Ap	Gl	Ap	Gl	Ap	Gl	Ap	Gl
18+11	7	4+2	3	5+1	1	0+3	0	0	0	27+17	11

CRAIG EASTMOND

Prem Lge		Europe		FA Cup		Lge Cup		C. Shield		Total	
Ap	Gl	Ap	Gl	Ap	Gl	Ap	Gl	Ap	Gl	Ap	Gl
0	0	1	0	0	0	1+1	0	0	0	2+1	0

JAY EMMANUEL-THOMAS

Prem Lge		Europe		FA Cup		Lge Cup		C. Shield		Total	
Ap	Gl	Ap	Gl	Ap	Gl	Ap	Gl	Ap	Gl	Ap	Gl
0+1	0	0+1	0	0	0	0+2	0	0	0	0+4	0

CONOR HENDERSON

Prem Lge		Europe		FA Cup		Lge Cup		C. Shield		Total	
Ap	Gl	Ap	Gl	Ap	Gl	Ap	Gl	Ap	Gl	Ap	Gl
0	0	0	0	1	0	0	0	0	0	1	0

HENRI LANSBURY

Prem Lge		Europe		FA Cup		Lge Cup		C. Shield		Total	
Ap	Gl	Ap	Gl	Ap	Gl	Ap	Gl	Ap	Gl	Ap	Gl
0	0	0	0	0	0	1	1	0	0	1	1

IGNASI MIQUEL

Prem Lge		Europe		FA Cup		Lge Cup		C. Shield		Total	
Ap	Gl	Ap	Gl	Ap	Gl	Ap	Gl	Ap	Gl	Ap	Gl
0	0	0	0	2	0	0	0	0	0	2	0

NICKLAS BENDTNER

Prem Lge		Europe		FA Cup		Lge Cup		C. Shield		Total	
Ap	Gl	Ap	Gl	Ap	Gl	Ap	Gl	Ap	Gl	Ap	Gl
3+14	2	2+3	0	5	4	4+1	3	0	0	14+18	9

WOJCIECH SZCZESNY

Prem Lge		Europe		FA Cup		Lge Cup		C. Shield		Total	
Ap	Gl	Ap	Gl	Ap	Gl	Ap	Gl	Ap	Gl	Ap	Gl
15	0	2	0	2	0	5	0	0	0	24	0

Robin Van Persie
10

Name: Robin van Persie

Born: August 06, 1983
Rotterdam, Netherlands

Squad Number: 10

Position: Striker

Previous Club: Feyenoord

Joined Gunners:
May 17, 2004

He is still such a speedy, skilful and alert striker that it is easy to forget that Robin is now in his late twenties, and therefore approaching what should be the prime of his playing career. What a star he is: the Dutchman is a deadly goal-taker, a productive goal-maker and is accurate from set-pieces. So many magical memories from his Gunners career to date: from his thumping winner against Charlton Athletic in 2006, his double against Blackburn Rovers in the previous year's FA Cup Final, and numerous goals, flicks and free-kicks since. He trains and prepares hard for matches, and the rewards of that work are evident for all to see.

Although injury has often hampered campaigns for the Rotterdam-born hitman, when he is on the pitch there can be no doubting his class. Long may he grace Emirates Stadium.

Andrey Arshavin

23

Arsène Wenger says:

'If you look at the assists in the Premier League, Arshavin is the best. He is a great player: his attitude is fantastic and his ability cannot be doubted. He analyses very well, is very honest and has a fantastic objective assessment of his own performance. He is very demanding for himself so I have a huge respect for him."

The Russian arrived in North London after a lengthy transfer saga. He quickly showed he had been well worth the wait. His versatility, technical know-how and sublime skills make him a monstrously important member of the Gunners squad.

Whether on the wings or straight through the middle, Arshavin terrifies opponents as much as he delights his own fans and team-mates. He links well with his fellow Gunners and seems to have an almost instinctive understanding of where they are and what they need. It is a delight to watch them connect.

The highlight of his 2010/11 season was his winning goal against Barcelona in the UEFA Champions League. It is a rare player who can score against the Spanish legends. His late, curled effort was a wonder goal in any circumstances. The fact it was the winner against such illustrious opponents says all you need to know about this fearless, fantastic star.

Andrey says: "When I retire I want to be remembered as a small Russian guy who did some magic things where people did not understand how he did it."

51

Trivia Quiz

Starting at the Back

1 Which goalkeeper returned to the Club for a second spell during 2010/11?
2 Which club did Carl Jenkinson join the Gunners from?
3 Laurent Koscielny qualifies to play for France and which other nation?
4 Which West London club did Wojciech Szczesny spend time on loan at?
5 What nationality is Lukasz Fabianski?
6 What is the name of Arsenal's long-term French right-back?
7 Thomas Vermaelen joined the Gunners from which Dutch giant?
8 Against which team did Arsenal get their first Premier League clean sheet in 2010/11?
9 At which team did Kieran Gibbs spend time on loan in 2008?
10 What nationality is Jens Lehmann: German or Australian?

Middle Class

1 Where was Emmanuel Frimpong born.
2 Which Czech midfielder was once absent through injury for 18 months?
3 Which midfielder represented Cameroon at the 2010 World Cup Finals?
4 In which year did Tomas Rosicky join the Gunners?
5 True or false: Aaron Ramsey is Irish.
6 In which season did Craig Eastmond make his first-team debut?
7 Which nation did Abou Diaby represent at the 2010 World Cup?
8 Which team did Jack Wilshere spend time on-loan at?
9 And which team did Wilshere make his Arsenal debut against?
10 What nationality is Andrey Arshavin?

On the Attack

1. Theo Walcott was born in which month: March or November?
2. Which Gunner was Theo's boyhood hero?
3. What nationality is Gervinho?
4. Marouane Chamakh scored on his home League debut against which team?
5. Which team did Robin van Persie score his debut Gunners goal against?
6. And in what year did the Dutchman join the Club?
7. Which Gunners striker has written four football books for children?
8. How many Premier League matches had Theo Walcott appeared in for Arsenal when he was included in the 2006 World Cup squad?
9. How many goals did the Gunners score in 2010/11?
10. What was the Club's goal difference?

History

1. In what year did Arsenal win the European Cup Winners' Cup?
2. Arsenal won the double in 1971. Which team did they beat in the FA Cup Final?
3. What is the name of the Scotsman who managed Arsenal between 1986 and 1995?
4. Against which team did Dennis Bergkamp score his famous 1997 hat-trick?
5. Arsenal won the FA Cup in 2002 and 2003. How many other times had the Club retained the trophy?
6. What nationality is Thierry Henry?
7. Name the team that Arsenal beat in the 1993 FA Cup Final and League Cup Final.
8. What was the official name of the stadium the Club lived in prior to Emirates?
9. In what year did Arsenal win its first FA Cup?
10. And who were their opponents?

The Boss

1. In what year was Mr Wenger born? 1949 or 1967.
2. Arsenal won the league and which other trophy in 1998?
3. Which country was the Manager working in prior to joining the Club?
4. Mr Wenger has never won the League Cup for Arsenal: true or false?
5. How many 'doubles' has he won for the Club?
6. Name one of the three teams that Mr Wenger played for.
7. How many languages is he fluent in: four or five?
8. He was voted 'Manager of the Year' in 1998, 2002 and which other year?
9. Mr Wenger guided the Club through an unbeaten league campaign in 2003/04. How many other managers have achieved this in English football?
10. Which country was he born in?

Answers on page 61.

CAMPING AT EMIRATES!

Four hundred members of Arsenal's young supporters club, the Junior Gunners, participated in Camping on the Pitch at the Gunners' home on Saturday, May 21.

Having won the chance to attend by entering a competition open to members only, the boys and girls aged seven to twelve years of age got to play on the pitch in matches organised by the Club's Community coaches before eating up at the exclusive Club Level.

After watching Gunners' Greatest Goals and a few games of table football the JGs bedded down for the night in the 200 two-person tents put out on the award-winning pitch in

NERS

TAKING THE BRITANNIA BY STORM!

A group of 90 Junior Gunners followed the team to Stoke City for the match in May. Although the result was not what had been hoped for, the young fans had a day to remember for their whole lives. They even met the Manager, Arsène Wenger! They also enjoyed fun quizzes on the coach journey, and they were featured on Arsenal Player. Junior Gunner Nick Wilson said: 'The highlight of the day was definitely when Jens Lehmann, the 'Invincible' goalkeeper and Arsène Wenger, our most successful manager ever, came out to sign our shirts, programmes and caps!'

HOW EGG-CITING!

On April 14, 150 Junior Gunners searched Emirates Stadium on the hunt for Easter Eggs. The eggs had been hidden in a number of special places around the stadium, which meant the navigational skills of the Junior Gunners were tested. They were helped with a special map featuring cryptic clues. Also on hand were an Easter Bunny and Easter Chick who handed out goodies. In addition, all 150 JGs were also treated to a special question and answer session with Tomas Rosicky and James Shea at the JG Forum.

a star formation, with mascot Gunnersaurus making sure everyone was tucked in.

A little rain helped wake all the boys and girls up bright and early Sunday morning, and it was time to pack up the tents and head back to the Royal Oak Suite for breakfast before attendees were picked up by their parents.

The Season in Photos!

Sometimes photographs tell a story better than words.
Here is the story of 2010/11 in photos.

The 2010/11 team photocall

Chamakh bulges the net v Wolves

Celebrating victory over Barcelona at Emirates

The return of Jens Lehmann

Winning goalscorer Aaron Ramsey salutes the crowd v Manchester United

Robin Van Persie celebrates scoring v Liverpool

Lining up at the Nou Camp

57

Charting The Progress...

Here you can refer back to key milestones in the 2010/11 season and keep track of the equivalent moments in the 2011/12 campaign. Enjoy!

Premier League

	2010/11	2011/12
Final position	Fourth	
First home win	v Blackpool 6-0	
First away win	v Blackburn 2-1	
First home draw	v Manchester City 0-0	
First home defeat	v WBA 2-3	
First away defeat	v Chelsea, 0-2	

Domestic Cups

FA Cup	Sixth round: Manchester United	
Carling Cup	Runners-up: Birmingham City	

Champions League

Progress	Knockout: Barcelona	
First home win	v Braga 6-0	
First away win	v Partizan Belgrade 3-1	
First home draw	None	
First away draw	None	
First home defeat	None	
First away defeat	v Shakhtar Donetsk 1-2	

First goals in...

Premier League	Walcott v Blackpool	
FA Cup	Fabregas v Leeds United	
Carling Cup	Lansbury v Tottenham Hotspur	

Quiz Answers

TRIVIA ANSWERS p52-53

Starting At The Back
1. Jens Lehmann
2. Charlton Athletic
3. Poland
4. Brentford
5. Polish
6. Bacary Sagna
7. Ajax
8. Blackpool
9. Norwich City
10. German

Middle Class
1. Ghana
2. Tomas Rosicky
3. Alex Song
4. 2006
5. False, he is Welsh
6. 2009/10
7. France
8. Bolton Wanderers
9. Blackburn Rovers
10. Russian

On The Attack
1. March
2. Thierry Henry
3. Ivorian
4. Blackpool
5. Manchester City
6. 2004
7. Theo Walcott
8. None
9. 72
10. +29

History
1. 1994
2. Liverpool
3. George Graham
4. Leicester City
5. Never
6. French
7. Sheffield Wednesday
8. Arsenal Stadium
9. 1930
10. Huddersfield Town

The Boss
1. 1949
2. FA Cup
3. Japan
4. True
5. Two
6. Mutzig, Mulhouse, Strasbourg
7. Five
8. 2004
9. None
10. France

CROSSWORD ANSWERS p42

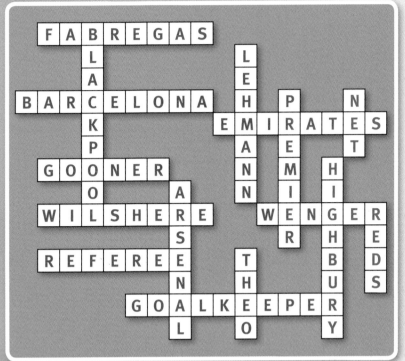

SPOT THE BALL ANSWER p43

Where's Gunnersaurus?